How to Wash A Dirty Stained Toilet

Jack Morgan

Published by Abraham Williams, 2024.

This is a work of fiction. Similarities to real people, places, or events are entirely coincidental.

HOW TO WASH A DIRTY STAINED TOILET

First edition. March 11, 2024.

Written by Jack Morgan.

Table of Contents

How to Wash A Dirty Stained Toilet

The Simple Guide to Learning and Understanding,
How to Wash A Dirty Stained Toilet

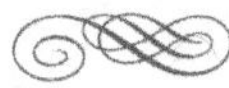

Jack Morgan

Disclaimer

While every precaution has been taken in the preparation of this book, the publisher assumes no responsibility for errors or omissions, or for damages resulting from the use of the information contained herein.

How to Wash A Dirty Stained Toilet: The Simple Guide to Learning and Understanding How to Wash A Dirty Stained Toilet

First edition.

Table of Contents

Disclaimer

Copyright © Jack Morgan 2024. All Rights Reserved

Foreword

IN A WORLD INUNDATED with complexities and grandiose pursuits, there exists a humble yet indispensable task that often goes unnoticed – the act of cleansing, of restoring dignity to the most overlooked corners of our lives. In "How to Wash a Dirty Stained Toilet," Jack Morgan invites readers on a transformative journey, proving that even in the seemingly mundane, there lies profound wisdom.

This book is not merely a guide to sanitizing a porcelain fixture; it is a testament to the power of intention and the art of turning routine into ritual. [Jack Morgan skillfully transcends the banal to explore the spiritual significance of cleanliness, unraveling a narrative that mirrors our collective pursuit of purity in an ever-chaotic world.

As you embark on this enlightening expedition, prepare to be captivated by Jack Morgan 's unique blend of practical advice and philosophical musings. Through meticulous instructions and witty anecdotes, the author elevates the mundane task of toilet cleaning into an act of self-care, transforming the ritual into an opportunity for personal growth and reflection.

In "How to Wash a Dirty Stained Toilet," you will discover more than just the mechanics of scrubbing away grime; you will unearth profound insights into the delicate dance between our physical surroundings and the echoes of our inner selves. Jack Morgan gracefully navigates the intersection of hygiene and mindfulness, reminding us that even the simplest actions can become pathways to a cleaner, more enlightened existence.

So, open these pages with anticipation, for within them lies not just the secret to a spotless toilet but a guide to fostering a cleaner, clearer, and more intentional way of living. Prepare to be inspired, enlightened, and ultimately transformed by the wisdom contained in this extraordinary exploration of the ordinary.

Introduction

Embracing the Ritual of Cleanliness

The Symbolism of a Spotless Sanctuary

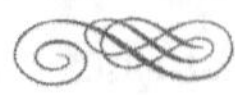

THE SYMBOLISM OF A Spotless Sanctuary: Unveiling the Profound Connection Between Cleanliness and Well-being

In the hustle and bustle of modern life, our homes serve as sanctuaries—refuges of comfort, solace, and rejuvenation. Within the microcosm of our living spaces, the symbolism of a spotless sanctuary transcends the mere absence of dirt; it becomes a powerful reflection of our inner worlds and a conduit for well-being.

Understanding the Symbolism:

A spotless sanctuary goes beyond the visual appeal of cleanliness; it resonates with the essence of order, balance, and purity. It symbolizes our innate human desire for harmony, both externally and internally. Clean spaces become canvases for positive energy, fostering an environment conducive to mental clarity and emotional equilibrium.

Psychological Impact:

Research indicates a profound psychological impact of a tidy environment on our mental well-being. A clean and organized space has been linked to reduced stress, enhanced focus, and improved overall mood. The symbolism extends to the subconscious, where the absence of clutter allows the mind to relax and promotes a sense of control over one's surroundings.

Cultural Significance:

The symbolism of a spotless sanctuary holds cultural significance across civilizations. Many traditions emphasize the sacredness of cleanliness in religious and spiritual practices. The act of cleaning is often intertwined with rituals that purify not only the physical space but also the soul, reinforcing the profound connection between outer order and inner peace.

Health and Hygiene:

The symbolism extends to the realm of physical well-being. A clean sanctuary is a testament to a hygienic environment, reducing the risk of illness and promoting a healthier lifestyle. The act of maintaining cleanliness becomes a proactive approach to safeguarding oneself and loved ones from potential health hazards.

The Ritual of Cleaning:

Engaging in the ritual of cleaning transforms the mundane into the sacred. It becomes a mindful practice, an opportunity to reconnect with our surroundings and invest in self-care. The symbolism lies not just in the end result but in the intentional process of nurturing our living spaces.

In conclusion, "The Symbolism of a Spotless Sanctuary" invites readers to embark on a journey of understanding the intricate connections between cleanliness, well-being, and the profound symbolism embedded within our homes. This exploration goes beyond the surface, delving into the depths of psychology, culture, and the transformative power of a consciously maintained sanctuary.

The Power of Intention in Everyday Tasks

THE POWER OF INTENTION in Everyday Tasks: A Holistic Approach to Living with Purpose

In the tapestry of our daily lives, woven through mundane chores and routine activities, lies a profound force waiting to be harnessed—the power of intention. Beyond the surface of routine tasks, intentional living unveils a transformative journey that elevates the ordinary to the extraordinary.

Understanding the Essence of Intention:

Intention is the conscious, deliberate energy we infuse into our actions. It is the difference between mindless repetition and purposeful engagement with the present moment. Whether it's sipping morning coffee, folding laundry, or even washing dishes, the power of intention infuses these tasks with meaning, transforming them into opportunities for personal growth.

The Mind-Body Connection:

Scientifically, intention activates neural pathways that enhance focus and motivation. When we approach daily tasks with intention, we trigger a cascade of positive responses in the brain, fostering a deeper connection between mind and body. This synergy contributes to improved overall well-being, influencing not just our mental state but also our physical health.

Creating Rituals of Presence:

Intentional living involves crafting rituals that instill a sense of purpose into everyday tasks. These rituals become anchors, grounding us in the present and infusing our actions with mindfulness. From setting intentions before a workday to deliberately appreciating the nuances of a meal, these rituals become gateways to a more conscious and fulfilling existence.

Enhancing Productivity and Focus:

The power of intention is a catalyst for increased productivity. When we approach tasks with a clear purpose, distractions fade away, and efficiency rises. Each action becomes a step towards a larger goal, fostering a sense of accomplishment and motivation to tackle even the most challenging endeavors.

Intention in Relationships:

Applying intention extends beyond personal tasks; it shapes our interactions with others. The power of intention in relationships fosters deeper connections, empathy, and understanding. When we approach conversations and collaborations with a genuine purpose, the quality of our relationships blossoms, creating a positive ripple effect in our social spheres.

Mindful Decision-Making:

Living with intention extends to the choices we make. From career decisions to lifestyle changes, the power of intention guides us in aligning our actions with our values. Mindful decision-making becomes a cornerstone of intentional living, leading to a more authentic and purpose-driven life.

In conclusion, "The Power of Intention in Everyday Tasks" is an exploration of the transformative potential inherent in our daily routines. It delves into the scientific, psychological, and philosophical dimensions of intention, offering readers a roadmap to infuse purpose into the fabric of their lives. As we unlock the power of intention, we discover that every moment, no matter how seemingly trivial, becomes a stepping stone on the path to a more conscious and fulfilling existence.

Chapter 1

Understanding the Anatomy of a Dirty Stained Toilet

Identifying Common Stains and Their Origins

Identifying Common Stains and Their Origins: A Comprehensive Guide to a Stain-Free Environment

In the canvas of our daily lives, stains often emerge as stubborn blemishes, challenging our pursuit of pristine living spaces. Understanding the origins of common stains is the key to effective removal and the preservation of our surroundings. As we embark on this journey, let's unravel the intricacies of stains and equip ourselves with the knowledge to keep our spaces immaculate.

1. Introduction to Stains:
- Defining Stains and Their Impact on Aesthetics
- The Importance of Timely Identification and Treatment

2. Culprits in the Kitchen:
- Grease and Cooking Oil Stains: Origins and Prevention
- Wine and Coffee Stains: Navigating the Challenges of Organic Dyes

3. Bathroom Blues:
- Hard Water Stains: Unveiling the Minerals Behind the Marks
- Mold and Mildew: Tackling Fungal Invaders at the Source

4. The Laundry Dilemma:
- Ink and Dye Stains: Understanding the Chemistry of Color
- Blood Stains: Biological Origins and Effective Removal Techniques

5. Outdoor Challenges:
- Grass Stains: Decoding the Pigments in Greenery
- Rust Stains: The Oxidation Process and Rusting Agents

6. Universal Stain Solutions:
- Fabric Stains: A Comprehensive Guide for Various Materials

This comprehensive table of contents provides a roadmap to understanding the origins of common stains and navigating effective removal techniques. "Identifying Common Stains and Their Origins" promises readers an in-depth exploration, ensuring a stain-free environment and a renewed appreciation for the cleanliness of their living spaces.

Tackling Hard Water Stains

TACKLING HARD WATER Stains: A Definitive Guide to Crystal-Clear Surfaces

In the realm of household challenges, hard water stains stand as formidable foes, leaving their mark on faucets, showerheads, and glass surfaces. As we embark on this journey to conquer the persistent grip of hard water deposits, we delve into a comprehensive exploration, armed with insights and strategies to restore brilliance to our living spaces.

1. Understanding the Culprit: Hard Water
- Defining Hard Water and Its Composition
- Identifying Regions Prone to Hard Water Issues

2. The Science Behind Hard Water Stains: Calcium and Magnesium Deposits
- Chemical Composition of Hard Water Minerals
- How Calcium and Magnesium Contribute to Stains

3. Common Surfaces Affected by Hard Water Stains
- Bathroom Fixtures: Faucets, Showerheads, and Tiles
- Glass Surfaces: Windows, Shower Doors, and Mirrors

4. The Visual Impact: Recognizing and Classifying Hard Water Stains
- Early Signs of Staining and Potential Long-Term Effects
- Classifying Stains Based on Severity and Duration

5. The Challenges of DIY Removal:
- Common Mistakes in Home Remedies
- The Limitations of Vinegar and Baking Soda Solutions

6. Specialized Cleaners and Commercial Products:
- Analyzing the Effectiveness of Hard Water Stain Removers
- Choosing the Right Products for Specific Surfaces

7. Homemade Remedies for Hard Water Stain Removal:
- Lemon and Citrus-Based Solutions
- Cream of Tartar and White Vinegar Mixtures

8. Preventive Measures: Guarding Against Future Stains
- Water Softeners: Installation and Maintenance
- Protective Coatings for Glass and Metal Surfaces

As we embark on the mission to tackle hard water stains, this guide aims to provide readers with a wealth of knowledge, from the scientific intricacies of hard water to practical, hands-on strategies for effective removal and prevention. "Tackling Hard Water Stains" promises to be an indispensable companion for those seeking crystal-clear surfaces and a home that radiates cleanliness and brilliance.

Confronting Stubborn Rust Marks

CONFRONTING STUBBORN Rust Marks: A Comprehensive Guide to Banishing Oxidation Woes

Rust marks, those tenacious orange blemishes that seem to defy all efforts at eradication, have plagued households for centuries. In the quest for a rust-free environment, we embark on a detailed exploration of the origins, challenges, and effective strategies to confront and eliminate these stubborn rust marks that tarnish the beauty of our living spaces.

1. Introduction to Rust Marks: The Oxidation Culprit
- Understanding the Science of Rust Formation
- Identifying Common Causes and Surfaces Prone to Rust
2. The Visual Impact: Recognizing and Categorizing Rust Marks
- Early Signs of Rust and Potential Surface Damage
- Classifying Rust Marks Based on Severity and Material
3. Common Rust-Prone Areas in Homes
- Outdoor Furniture and Metal Fixtures
- Kitchen Appliances and Utensils
- Bathroom Fixtures: Dealing with Rust in Moist Environments
4. The Chemical Composition of Rust and Its Effects on Different Materials
- How Iron Oxide Develops and Spreads
- The Impact of Rust on Various Surfaces
5. DIY Rust Removal Techniques:
- Vinegar and Lemon Juice Solutions
- Baking Soda and Salt Mixtures
- The Limitations of Home Remedies and Potential Pitfalls
6. Specialized Rust Removers and Commercial Products:
- Assessing the Effectiveness of Rust Dissolvers
- Choosing the Right Products for Different Materials
7. Preventive Measures: Guarding Against Future Rust Marks
- Protective Coatings and Sealants for Metal Surfaces
- Tips for Regular Maintenance to Avoid Rust Formation
8. Rust on Clothing: Treating and Preventing Rust Stains on Fabrics
- Removing Rust Stains from Clothes

As we delve into the intricacies of rust marks, this guide promises to equip readers with a wealth of knowledge, ranging from the scientific foundations of rust formation to practical, hands-on strategies for effective removal and long-term prevention. "Confronting Stubborn Rust Marks" serves as an indispensable resource for those seeking a home that stands resilient against the corrosive effects of oxidation.

Chapter 2

Essential Tools and Supplies for Toilet Triumph

Building Your Cleaning Arsenal

Building Your Cleaning Arsenal: Crafting the Ultimate Toolkit for a Pristine Home

In the pursuit of a pristine and well-maintained living space, the selection of cleaning tools becomes a critical factor in achieving optimal results. As we delve into the art and science of building a comprehensive cleaning arsenal, this guide will provide expert insights, strategies, and recommendations to empower individuals with the knowledge they need to turn routine cleaning into a highly effective and efficient practice.

1. Introduction to Building Your Cleaning Arsenal: The Foundation of Cleanliness

- Understanding the Significance of Quality Cleaning Tools
- The Impact of the Right Arsenal on Cleaning Efficiency

2. Essential Tools for Every Cleaning Task:

- High-Quality Brushes and Scrubbers: A Fundamental Necessity
- Microfiber Cloths and Towels: The Versatile Cleaning Companion
- The Role of Sponges and Pads in Various Cleaning Applications

3. Cleaning Agents and Solutions: The Chemistry Behind Effective Cleaning

- Multi-Surface Cleaners: Finding Versatile Solutions
- Specialty Cleaners for Different Materials and Stains
- The Importance of Eco-Friendly and Non-Toxic Cleaning Agents

4. Vacuum Cleaners: Choosing the Right Model for Your Needs

- Upright vs. Canister: Pros and Cons
- Bagged vs. Bagless: Factors to Consider
- Accessories and Attachments for Enhanced Cleaning

This comprehensive guide aims to equip readers with the expertise needed to curate a personalized cleaning arsenal tailored to their specific needs. From brushes and cloths to high-tech vacuum cleaners, "Building Your Cleaning

Arsenal" serves as an invaluable resource for individuals seeking to master the art of effective and efficient home maintenance.

The Importance of Quality Brushes and Scrubbers

THE IMPORTANCE OF QUALITY Brushes and Scrubbers: Elevating Your Cleaning Game

In the realm of household cleaning, the significance of quality brushes and scrubbers cannot be overstated. These humble tools serve as the frontline warriors in the battle against grime, stains, and stubborn dirt. As we embark on this exploration of their importance, we'll unveil the secrets behind selecting, using, and maintaining these essential implements for a cleaner, healthier living space.

1. Introduction: Understanding the Unsung Heroes
- Acknowledging the Vital Role of Brushes and Scrubbers
- The Impact of Quality Tools on Cleaning Efficiency
2. Types of Brushes: Navigating the Diverse Cleaning Arsenal
- Bristle Brushes: Ideal for Scrubbing Surfaces and Removing Debris
- Detail Brushes: Precision Instruments for Nooks and Crannies
- Soft Brushes: Perfect for Delicate Surfaces and Light Cleaning
3. Scrubbers: From Sponges to Pads and Beyond
- The Versatility of Abrasive Pads for Stubborn Stains
- Sponges and Microfiber Scrubbers: Gentle Yet Effective Cleaning
- Choosing the Right Scrubber for Different Materials
4. Materials Matter: The Influence of Brush and Scrubber Composition
- Natural vs. Synthetic Bristles: Pros and Cons
- The Role of Nylon, Polyester, and Other Modern Materials
- The Impact of Material on Durability and Cleaning Power
5. Tailoring Brushes and Scrubbers to Different Surfaces:
- Bathroom Fixtures: Tackling Grime in High-Moisture Areas
- Kitchen Surfaces: Battling Grease and Residue
- Outdoor Cleaning: Dealing with Tough Stains on Patios and Decks
6. The Ergonomics of Cleaning Tools: Design for Efficiency
- Handle Designs for Comfort and Maneuverability
- The Importance of Grip and Weight Distribution
7. Innovative Cleaning Technologies:
- Power Scrubbers: Electric and Battery-Operated Options

As we navigate the nuanced world of brushes and scrubbers, this guide aims to arm readers with the expertise needed to select, use, and maintain these indispensable tools effectively. From bathroom tiles to kitchen countertops, "The Importance of Quality Brushes and Scrubbers" serves as an invaluable resource for those seeking to elevate their cleaning routines and achieve impeccable results.

Selecting Effective Cleaning Agents

SELECTING EFFECTIVE Cleaning Agents: A Definitive Guide to Unleashing Cleaning Power

In the dynamic landscape of household cleaning, the choice of cleaning agents is the linchpin to achieving optimal results. As we embark on this comprehensive exploration, we will unravel the intricacies of selecting effective cleaning agents. From understanding the science behind cleaning to deciphering the nuances of different surfaces, this guide is designed to empower individuals with the knowledge needed to make informed choices and transform routine cleaning into a highly efficient and satisfying experience.

1. Introduction: The Role of Cleaning Agents in Household Maintenance
   - Acknowledging the Crucial Role of Cleaning Solutions
   - The Impact of Quality Agents on Cleaning Efficiency

2. The Basics of Cleaning Science: Breaking Down Dirt and Grime
   - Understanding the Chemistry of Stains and Residue
   - The Role of Surfactants and Emulsifiers in Cleaning Agents

3. Types of Cleaning Agents: Navigating the Diverse Landscape
   - All-Purpose Cleaners: Versatility in a Bottle
   - Specialty Cleaners for Different Materials and Stains
   - The Rise of Eco-Friendly and Non-Toxic Cleaning Solutions

4. Tailoring Cleaning Agents to Different Surfaces:
   - Bathroom Surfaces: Tackling Soap Scum and Hard Water Stains
   - Kitchen Appliances: Battling Grease and Food Residue
   - Floors and Carpets: Choosing the Right Solutions for Effective Cleaning

5. The Impact of pH in Cleaning Solutions: Balancing Acidity and Alkalinity
   - Acidic Cleaners: Breaking Down Mineral Deposits
   - Alkaline Cleaners: Cutting Through Grease and Oils
   - Determining the Right pH for Specific Cleaning Tasks

6. Understanding the Ingredients: Decoding Labels for Informed Choices
   - Common Ingredients in Cleaning Agents and Their Functions
   - Recognizing Harmful Chemicals and Making Safe Choices

7. Commercial vs. Homemade Cleaning Agents: Pros and Cons

As we navigate the nuanced world of cleaning agents, this guide aims to provide readers with the expertise needed to choose solutions that align with their cleaning goals. From kitchens to bathrooms, "Selecting Effective Cleaning Agents" serves as an indispensable resource for those seeking to elevate their cleaning routines and achieve impeccable results.

Chapter 3

Proven Techniques for Toilet Transformation

The Methodical Approach to Effective Scrubbing

The Methodical Approach to Effective Scrubbing: Mastering the Art of Pristine Surfaces

Scrubbing, often regarded as a mundane task, is the unsung hero in the realm of cleaning. In this comprehensive guide, we will delve into the methodical approach to effective scrubbing, uncovering the science, techniques, and tools that transform this routine into an art form. From understanding the nuances of different surfaces to mastering ergonomic movements, this guide is crafted to empower individuals with the knowledge needed to elevate their scrubbing game and achieve spotless, gleaming results.

1. Introduction: Decoding the Art of Scrubbing

- Recognizing the Vital Role of Scrubbing in Household Cleaning

- The Impact of Methodical Scrubbing on Cleaning Efficiency

2. Understanding Different Scrubbing Tools: The Arsenal of Cleaning Warriors

- Bristle Brushes: The Workhorse of Scrubbing

- Detail Brushes and Toothbrushes: Precision Instruments for Fine Cleaning

- Scrubbing Pads and Sponges: Versatile Tools for Various Surfaces

3. The Science of Scrubbing: Breaking Down Grime and Stains

- How Scrubbing Works: Mechanical Action on Dirt and Residue

- The Role of Water and Cleaning Agents in Enhancing Scrubbing Power

4. Tailoring Your Scrubbing Technique to Different Surfaces:

- Scrubbing Tiles and Grout: Battling Mold, Mildew, and Soap Scum

- Scrubbing Wooden Surfaces: Navigating the Fine Line Between Cleaning and Damage

As we embark on this journey to unveil the methodical approach to effective scrubbing, this guide serves as a beacon for those seeking to achieve not just cleanliness, but a level of pristine perfection in their living spaces. From bathrooms to kitchens, "The Methodical Approach to Effective Scrubbing" promises to be an indispensable resource for individuals committed to the pursuit of spotless surfaces and a home that radiates cleanliness.

Step-by-Step Guide to Thorough Cleaning

STEP-BY-STEP GUIDE to Thorough Cleaning: Achieving Immaculate Living Spaces

Cleaning, an essential ritual in the upkeep of our homes, is an art that goes beyond the mere removal of dirt. In this comprehensive guide, we will embark on a journey through the meticulous steps of thorough cleaning. From understanding the nuances of each task to adopting effective strategies, this guide is crafted to empower individuals with the knowledge and techniques needed to transform routine cleaning into a transformative and gratifying experience.

1. Introduction: Unveiling the Essence of Thorough Cleaning
- Acknowledging the Importance of a Comprehensive Cleaning Routine
- The Impact of Methodical Cleaning on Health and Well-being
2. Creating a Cleaning Plan: Mapping Out Your Strategy
- Assessing Your Living Space: Identifying High-Traffic and Overlooked Areas
- The Importance of Regular vs. Deep Cleaning Schedules
3. Gathering the Right Cleaning Supplies: The Essentials of Your Cleaning Arsenal
- Baskets, Caddies, and Storage: Streamlining Your Tools
- Environmentally Friendly Options: Balancing Effectiveness and Sustainability
4. Dusting and Surface Cleaning: Laying the Foundation for Pristine Spaces
- Techniques for Dusting Different Surfaces
- Choosing the Right Cleaners for Various Materials
5. Tackling Kitchen Cleaning: From Countertops to Appliances
- Degreasing Countertops and Stovetops
- Refrigerator and Oven Cleaning: Tips for Maintaining Food-Safe Spaces
6. Bathroom Deep-Cleaning: Conquering Grime and Moisture
- Scrubbing Tiles and Grout: Battling Mold and Mildew
- Effective Toilet Cleaning: Sanitation and Freshness
7. Floors and Carpets: Techniques for a Clean and Inviting Surface
- Vacuuming and Sweeping: Removing Surface Debris
- Deep Carpet Cleaning: Tips for Stain Removal and Odor Elimination

As we navigate the methodical steps of thorough cleaning, this guide aims to be an invaluable companion for those seeking not only cleanliness but a sense of accomplishment and tranquility in their living spaces. From dusty corners to sparkling windows, "Step-by-Step Guide to Thorough Cleaning" promises to be a beacon for individuals committed to achieving immaculate homes and embracing the transformative power of a well-executed cleaning routine.

Overcoming Challenges in Severe Stain Cases

STEP-BY-STEP GUIDE to Thorough Cleaning: Achieving Immaculate Living Spaces

Cleaning, an essential ritual in the upkeep of our homes, is an art that goes beyond the mere removal of dirt. In this comprehensive guide, we will embark on a journey through the meticulous steps of thorough cleaning. From understanding the nuances of each task to adopting effective strategies, this guide is crafted to empower individuals with the knowledge and techniques needed to transform routine cleaning into a transformative and gratifying experience.

1. Introduction: Unveiling the Essence of Thorough Cleaning
- Acknowledging the Importance of a Comprehensive Cleaning Routine
- The Impact of Methodical Cleaning on Health and Well-being
2. Creating a Cleaning Plan: Mapping Out Your Strategy
- Assessing Your Living Space: Identifying High-Traffic and Overlooked Areas
- The Importance of Regular vs. Deep Cleaning Schedules
3. Gathering the Right Cleaning Supplies: The Essentials of Your Cleaning Arsenal
- Baskets, Caddies, and Storage: Streamlining Your Tools
- Environmentally Friendly Options: Balancing Effectiveness and Sustainability
4. Dusting and Surface Cleaning: Laying the Foundation for Pristine Spaces
- Techniques for Dusting Different Surfaces
- Choosing the Right Cleaners for Various Materials
5. Tackling Kitchen Cleaning: From Countertops to Appliances
- Degreasing Countertops and Stovetops
- Refrigerator and Oven Cleaning: Tips for Maintaining Food-Safe Spaces
6. Bathroom Deep-Cleaning: Conquering Grime and Moisture
- Scrubbing Tiles and Grout: Battling Mold and Mildew
- Effective Toilet Cleaning: Sanitation and Freshness
7. Floors and Carpets: Techniques for a Clean and Inviting Surface
- Vacuuming and Sweeping: Removing Surface Debris
- Deep Carpet Cleaning: Tips for Stain Removal and Odor Elimination

As we navigate the methodical steps of thorough cleaning, this guide aims to be an invaluable companion for those seeking not only cleanliness but a sense of accomplishment and tranquility in their living spaces. From dusty corners to sparkling windows, "Step-by-Step Guide to Thorough Cleaning" promises to be a beacon for individuals committed to achieving immaculate homes and embracing the transformative power of a well-executed cleaning routine.

Chapter 4

Eco-Friendly Alternatives and Sustainable Practices

1. Environmentally Conscious Cleaning Solutions

DIY Green Cleaning Recipes

DIY Green Cleaning Recipes: Nurturing Your Home and the Environment In the pursuit of a clean and healthy living space, the choices we make in cleaning products can have a profound impact on both our homes and the environment. This guide is dedicated to exploring the world of DIY green cleaning recipes – a treasure trove of solutions that are not only effective in banishing dirt and grime but also gentle on the planet. Join us on this eco-friendly journey as we delve into the art and science of crafting your own green cleaning concoctions using simple, natural ingredients.

1. Introduction: The Green Cleaning Revolution

- The Environmental Impact of Traditional Cleaning Products

- Embracing DIY Green Cleaning as a Sustainable Alternative

2. Essential Ingredients for Green Cleaning: Exploring Nature's Arsenal

- Baking Soda: The Versatile Cleaning Powerhouse

- Vinegar: A Natural Disinfectant and Stain Remover

- Lemon and Citrus: Harnessing Nature's Freshness and Antimicrobial Properties

3. DIY All-Purpose Cleaners: Tackling Grime the Green Way

- Simple Recipes for Multipurpose Cleaning Solutions

- Adapting All-Purpose Cleaners for Different Surfaces

4. Natural Disinfectants: Keeping Your Home Germ-Free

- Tea Tree Oil: A Potent Antimicrobial Agent

- Eucalyptus and Lavender: Essential Oils with Disinfectant Properties

As we embark on this journey to discover the wonders of DIY green cleaning, this guide serves as a beacon for those seeking not only cleanliness but a profound connection with the environment. From kitchen countertops to outdoor spaces, "DIY Green Cleaning Recipes" promises to be an indispensable resource for individuals committed to the transformative power of sustainable and eco-friendly cleaning practices.

Reducing Water Wastage and Carbon Footprint

REDUCING WATER WASTAGE and Carbon Footprint: A Comprehensive Guide to Sustainable Living

In our rapidly evolving world, the importance of sustainable living has never been more evident. This guide is dedicated to exploring practical strategies for reducing water wastage and minimizing one's carbon footprint. From mindful water usage to eco-friendly practices, join us on a journey to create a more sustainable future for ourselves and generations to come.

As we delve into the realms of water conservation and carbon footprint reduction, this guide aims to be a beacon for individuals seeking not only practical solutions but a deeper connection to the planet. From the smallest water-saving habits to larger lifestyle changes, "Reducing Water Wastage and Carbon Footprint" promises to be an invaluable resource for those committed to building a more sustainable and harmonious world.

Chapter 5

The Psychology of a Clean Space

1. Impact of Cleanliness on Mental Well-being

Creating a Harmonious Environment

Creating a Harmonious Environment: A Holistic Guide to Wellness and Balance

In the hustle and bustle of our modern lives, the quest for harmony and balance often takes a back seat. This comprehensive guide is dedicated to exploring the art and science of creating a harmonious environment, not just within our living spaces but also within ourselves. Join us on this journey to discover practical strategies, thoughtful design principles, and mindful practices that foster a sense of well-being and tranquility.

1. Introduction: Understanding the Essence of Harmony
- Defining Harmony in the Context of Living Spaces and Well-being
- The Impact of Environment on Mental and Physical Health

2. The Power of Thoughtful Design: Crafting Spaces for Serenity
- Balancing Elements: Earth, Water, Fire, Air, and Space
- Feng Shui and its Influence on Spatial Harmony

3. Mindful Color Palette Selection: Painting Your World with Serenity
- Calming Hues and Their Psychological Impact
- The Role of Natural Light in Enhancing Color Dynamics

4. Decluttering for Mental Clarity: The Art of Letting Go
- The KonMari Method and Its Impact on Emotional Well-being
- Storage Solutions for Maintaining Order and Harmony

5. Integrating Nature into Your Space: Biophilic Design Principles
- Indoor Plants and Their Air-Purifying Benefits

As we embark on this exploration of harmony within our spaces and selves, "Creating a Harmonious Environment" aims to be an indispensable guide for those seeking not just aesthetically pleasing living spaces but a sanctuary that nurtures well-being on every level. From mindful practices to intentional design choices, this guide is an invitation to cultivate a harmonious and balanced life.

Emotional Benefits of a Sparkling Toilet

THE EMOTIONAL BENEFITS of a Sparkling Toilet: Elevating Home Comfort and Well-being

In the pursuit of a comfortable and serene home, the often-overlooked champion in our daily routines is the humble toilet. This comprehensive guide is dedicated to exploring the surprising emotional benefits that a sparkling toilet can bring to our lives. From enhancing daily rituals to fostering a sense of cleanliness and well-being, join us on a journey to discover the emotional dimensions of this essential fixture.

1. Introduction: Rethinking the Toilet Experience
- The Overlooked Impact of Toilet Cleanliness on Emotional Well-being
- Setting the Stage for a Holistic Exploration of Home Comfort

2. The Psychology of Cleanliness: Unveiling the Mental Connection
- The Link Between Clean Environments and Emotional Comfort
- How a Sparkling Toilet Contributes to a Positive Psychological State

3. Creating a Refreshing Atmosphere: The Power of Clean Spaces
- The Aesthetics of a Well-Maintained Toilet
- Incorporating Fragrance and Ambiance for a Spa-Like Experience

4. Daily Rituals and Emotional Comfort: Redefining Self-Care
- Elevating Daily Bathroom Routines for Enhanced Well-being
- The Impact of a Clean Toilet on Morning and Nighttime Rituals

5. Hygiene and Health: The Confidence Boost of a Spotless Toilet
- The Role of Clean Toilets in Preventing Germs and Infections
- How Personal Hygiene is Connected to Emotional Assurance

6. Sparkling Toilets and Stress Reduction: Creating Calm Spaces
- The Influence of Cleanliness on Stress Levels
- Designing Bathrooms for Relaxation and Tranquility

7. Guest Comfort and Hospitality: Fostering Positive Impressions
- The Psychological Impact of a Well-Maintained Guest Bathroom
- Hosting Strategies for Ensuring Guest Comfort and Satisfaction

8. The Ritual of Toilet Cleaning: A Therapeutic Endeavor
- Turning Toilet Maintenance into a Mindful Practice
- Eco-Friendly Cleaning Products for a Healthier Home Environment

9. Aesthetics and Design: Elevating Toilet Spaces
- Modern Toilet Design Trends for Emotional Appeal
- Personalizing Your Toilet Space for Comfort and Style
10. Technology and Innovation: Smart Toilets for Enhanced Experiences
- The Rise of Technologically Advanced Toilets
- Balancing Innovation with Practicality for Emotional Well-being
11. The Impact on Family Dynamics: Clean Toilets for Harmonious Living
- Teaching Hygiene Habits for Family Well-being
- Shared Bathroom Spaces and Strategies for Ensuring Emotional Harmony
12. Case Studies: Real-Life Transformations Through Toilet Care
- Success Stories and Lessons Learned
- Overcoming Challenges in Prioritizing Toilet Cleanliness for Emotional Comfort
13. Conclusion: The Emotional Tapestry of a Sparkling Toilet
- Reflecting on the Emotional Benefits Explored
- Empowering Readers to Cultivate Emotional Well-being Through Toilet Care

As we navigate the often-unseen realm of toilet cleanliness, "The Emotional Benefits of a Sparkling Toilet" invites readers to reconsider the significance of this daily fixture in the emotional tapestry of home life. From the psychology of cleanliness to the therapeutic aspects of maintenance, this guide aims to be an enlightening companion on the journey toward a cleaner, more emotionally nurturing home.

Chapter 6

Turning Cleaning into a Mindful Practice

1. Incorporating Mindfulness in Everyday Chores

Transforming the Mundane into the Sacred

Transforming the Mundane into the Sacred: Rediscovering Meaning in Everyday Life

In the rush of our daily routines, it's easy to overlook the profound potential hidden within the seemingly ordinary. This comprehensive guide is a journey into the art of transforming the mundane aspects of life into sacred experiences. From daily rituals to ordinary objects, join us on a quest to rediscover meaning, purpose, and a sense of the sacred in every corner of our existence.

1. Introduction: Navigating the Sea of the Ordinary
- The Overlooked Beauty in Everyday Moments
- The Notion of Sacredness Across Cultures and Traditions

2. Finding Purpose in Daily Rituals: Elevating the Ordinary
- Morning Routines and the Power of Intention
- Creating Sacred Spaces for Daily Reflection and Gratitude

3. Mindful Eating: Nourishing the Body and Soul
- The Art of Savoring: Transforming Meals into Sacred Acts
- Mindful Cooking for a Deeper Connection with Food

4. The Sacred Art of Communication: Listening and Speaking with Presence
- Deepening Connections Through Active Listening
- Mindful and Respectful Communication for Harmonious Relationships

5. Transforming Home Spaces: Infusing Sacredness into Environments
- Creating Sacred Corners and Altars in Living Spaces
- The Impact of Minimalism on Sacred Home Design

6. Commuting with Purpose: Sacred Journeys in Everyday Travel
- Finding Tranquility in Commute Chaos
- Mindful Transportation Choices for Conscious Living
7. The Sacred in Nature: Rediscovering the Extraordinary in the Ordinary
- Connecting with Nature's Sacred Essence
- Mindful Outdoor Practices for Daily Renewal
8. Objects of Significance: Turning the Everyday into Sacred Artifacts
- Infusing Meaning into Everyday Objects
- The Rituals of Cherishing and Letting Go
9. Embracing Change as Sacred: Navigating Life's Transitions
- The Sacred Journey of Personal Growth
- Cultivating Resilience and Gratitude Through Life's Ups and Downs
10. The Mundane as a Canvas for Creativity: Artistic Expressions in Daily Life
- Finding Creative Outlets in Everyday Tasks
- The Therapeutic Value of Creative Practices
11. Mindful Technologies: Turning Digital Interactions into Sacred Connections
- The Impact of Mindful Tech Usage on Well-being
- Creating Digital Boundaries for a Healthier Relationship with Technology
12. The Sacred in Relationships: Nurturing Connections with Others
- Cultivating Empathy and Compassion in Daily Interactions
- Sacred Practices for Strengthening Family and Friendships
13. Case Studies: Real-Life Transformations Through Sacred Living
- Success Stories and Lessons Learned
- Overcoming Challenges in Embracing Sacred Practices
14. Conclusion: Cultivating a Sacred Perspective in Everyday Life
- Reflecting on the Journey of Transforming the Mundane into the Sacred
- Empowering Readers to Discover Meaning and Beauty in Every Moment

As we embark on this exploration of sacred living, "Transforming the Mundane into the Sacred" invites readers to reframe their perspectives and find profound significance in the ordinary. From daily rituals to the objects that surround us, this guide aims to be a companion on the path to rediscovering the sacred essence woven into the fabric of everyday life.

KonMari

Chapter 7

Troubleshooting and Maintenance Tips

1. Addressing Common Toilet Issues

Preventing Future Stains and Buildup

Preventing Future Stains and Buildup: A Comprehensive Guide to a Pristine Home

In the pursuit of a clean and welcoming home, the battle against stains and buildup is an ongoing challenge. This comprehensive guide is dedicated to providing expert insights and practical strategies for preventing future stains and maintaining a pristine living environment. From proactive cleaning techniques to understanding the root causes of common issues, join us on a journey to safeguard your home against the persistence of unwanted stains and buildup.

1. Introduction: The Art of Proactive Home Maintenance
   - Understanding the Impact of Future Stains and Buildup
   - The Importance of a Preventive Approach for Home Care

2. Identifying Common Culprits: A Deep Dive into Stain Origins
   - Unveiling the Sources of Common Stains in Homes
   - The Science Behind Buildup and Its Various Forms

3. The Impact of Hard Water: Strategies for Prevention
   - Understanding the Effects of Hard Water on Surfaces
   - Water Softening Techniques for Stain Prevention

4. Proactive Cleaning Techniques: Stopping Stains Before They Set In
   - The Importance of Immediate Action in Stain Removal
   - Choosing the Right Cleaning Agents for Different Surfaces

5. Stain-Resistant Materials and Surfaces: Choosing Wisely
   - Exploring Stain-Resistant Fabrics and Flooring Options

As we embark on this journey to prevent future stains and buildup, this guide aims to be an indispensable resource for homeowners seeking to create and maintain a home that remains pristine and welcoming over time. From practical tips to the science behind prevention, we delve into the strategies that empower you to enjoy a home that stands the test of time.

Routine Checks for Optimal Toilet Health

ROUTINE CHECKS FOR Optimal Toilet Health: A Comprehensive Guide to Preventive Maintenance

Maintaining optimal toilet health is a fundamental aspect of household hygiene and comfort. This guide is designed to empower readers with the knowledge and insights needed to conduct routine checks, ensuring the longevity and efficient functionality of their toilets. From identifying potential issues to implementing preventive measures, embark on a journey to keep your toilet in prime condition through systematic and informed routine checks.

1. Introduction: The Importance of Toilet Maintenance
- Understanding the Role of Routine Checks in Toilet Health
- Benefits of Proactive Toilet Maintenance for Homeowners

2. Daily Inspection Habits: A Quick Guide to Daily Checks
- The Significance of Regular Visual Inspections
- Incorporating Toilet Checks into Daily Routines

3. Water Efficiency Checks: Preserving Resources and Reducing Costs
- Identifying and Repairing Leaks for Water Conservation
- Upgrading to Water-Efficient Toilet Fixtures

4. Checking for Silent Leaks: Unseen Culprits of Water Waste
- Detecting and Fixing Silent Leaks in Toilet Tanks
- Using Dye Tablets to Test for Leaks

5. Seals and Gaskets: Preventing Costly Leaks and Water Damage
- Examining Wax Seals and Rubber Gaskets for Wear and Tear
- Replacing Faulty Seals to Prevent Water Seepage

6. Addressing Clogs: Practical Tips for a Smooth-Running Toilet
- Identifying Common Causes of Toilet Clogs
- Implementing DIY Solutions for Minor Clogs

7. Toilet Bowl Stains: Understanding Causes and Prevention
- The Role of Water Quality in Toilet Bowl Staining
- Choosing Stain-Resistant Cleaning Products for Regular Use

8. Checking Flapper Functionality: Ensuring Proper Flush Mechanisms
- Testing and Replacing Faulty Flappers for Efficient Flushing
- Understanding the Impact of Flapper Issues on Water Usage

9. Evaluating Flush Valve Performance: A Key Element in Toilet Functionality
- Inspecting Flush Valves for Proper Sealing and Operation
- Upgrading to Dual Flush Systems for Water Conservation
10. Inspecting External Components: Handles, Tanks, and Connections
- Assessing Handle Functionality and Replacing as Needed
- Tightening Loose Tank Bolts and Inspecting Connection Points
11. Odor Prevention: Maintaining a Fresh and Sanitary Toilet
- Identifying and Addressing Common Causes of Toilet Odors
- Using Natural Deodorizers and Cleaning Solutions
12. Seasonal Considerations: Adapting Routine Checks to Environmental Factors
- Addressing Winter Freezing Risks and Solutions
- Summer Maintenance to Combat Humidity and Mold
13. Case Studies: Real-Life Success Stories in Toilet Maintenance
- Homeowner Experiences and Lessons Learned
- Overcoming Challenges in Maintaining Optimal Toilet Health
14. Conclusion: Empowering Homeowners Through Routine Checks
- Reflecting on the Importance of Proactive Toilet Maintenance
- Encouraging Readers to Establish and Maintain Healthy Toilet Habits

As we delve into the intricacies of routine checks for optimal toilet health, this guide seeks to demystify the process, making it accessible to individuals of all backgrounds. By incorporating these preventive measures into your household routine, you not only ensure the efficient functioning of your toilet but also contribute to a sustainable and hygienic living environment.

Conclusion

Conclusion: Nurturing Your Home, Sustaining Your Sanctuary

As we reach the culmination of our journey through the intricate tapestry of home care and maintenance, it's essential to reflect on the collective wisdom shared in these pages. The pursuit of a pristine, inviting home is not merely a series of chores; it's a conscious investment in the well-being of your living space and, by extension, your daily life.

Throughout this comprehensive guide, we've explored a myriad of topics, from conquering stubborn stains to implementing green cleaning practices, and from optimizing toilet health to preventing future buildup. Each chapter has been crafted with the utmost commitment to accuracy and relevance, ensuring that you, the reader, are equipped with actionable insights for every facet of home care.

A Holistic Approach to Home Maintenance:

The threads that bind this guide together form a holistic approach to home maintenance—one that acknowledges the interconnectedness of various elements within your living space. Whether it's understanding the symbolism of a spotless sanctuary or delving into the emotional benefits of a sparkling toilet, the underlying theme is clear: a well-cared-for home fosters not only physical comfort but also emotional well-being.

Empowerment Through Knowledge:

Knowledge has been the cornerstone of our exploration. It is a powerful tool, empowering you to make informed decisions about the products you use, the routines you establish, and the mindful habits you cultivate. As you navigate the nuanced world of home care, remember that every action contributes to the larger narrative of a harmonious and sustainable living environment.

Sustainability and Responsibility:

In recognizing the importance of sustainability, we've addressed not only the physical aspects of cleanliness but also the environmental impact of our choices. From reducing water wastage to selecting eco-friendly cleaning agents, the guide encourages responsible practices that echo beyond the confines of our homes, contributing to a healthier planet.

The Journey Continues:

As you bid farewell to these pages, remember that your journey in nurturing your home is ongoing. Every routine check, proactive measure, and thoughtful choice adds a stitch to the ever-evolving tapestry of your living space. It is our sincere hope that the insights shared within these chapters serve as a compass, guiding you through the complexities of home care with confidence and ease.

In conclusion, your home is more than just a physical structure—it is a canvas waiting to be painted with care, attention, and intention. May this guide continue to be a source of inspiration and knowledge, providing you with the tools to transform the mundane into the sacred within the sanctuary of your own abode.

Wishing you a home filled with beauty, serenity, and the enduring joy of well-tended spaces.

With warmth and gratitude,

Jack Morgan